This book is a must-read if you...

- are looking for wisdom

- believe that the world is one big classroom

- are searching for inspirational, witty one-liners

- want to know how others are inspired by quotes

- would love to learn how others are inspired

- wish to pause, reflect and grow

- are seeking daily motivation

- need a moment of contemplation

"I've just finished reading *The Little Book of Wolfie Wisdom* and I have to say, it's a brilliant read! It's very easy to read and full of useful, actionable insights into business and life. Highly recommended to anyone who wants to learn from the master of wisdom snippets".

Mike Cottam
Website Consultant, CottamWeb

"Colin has the ability to take you generously down memory lane. Wolfie's wisdom is so passionate, fun-filled, and laser-focused on making an impact with the reader. These one-liners and words of wisdom will be ingrained in your brain for life. This book is a must-read, and I guarantee will be a daily pick-me-up, and go-to for people when they're feeling a bit lost."

Lee Oughton
Kindness Crusader

"We all often hear these little phrases being banded about, right? In his *Little Book of Wolfie Wisdom*, Colin really captures super interesting insights and anecdotes that he shares with the reader. Not only that, he really captures how these sayings he's heard over the years have shaped his life, including his lengthy career in the police, and formerly the army.

This is the second book I've read of Colin's. I'd highly recommend both! This is something you can pick up, take a phrase that makes you think – and perhaps you can go away, implement and make some wonderful changes in your own life!"

Janine Mitchell MSc
Founder of Change for Success

THE LITTLE BOOK OF
WOLFIE WISDOM

COLIN TANSLEY

Author of Mastering the Wolf

First published in Great Britain in 2023
by Book Brilliance Publishing
265A Fir Tree Road, Epsom, Surrey, KT17 3LF
+44 (0)20 8641 5090
www.bookbrilliancepublishing.com
admin@bookbrilliancepublishing.com

A CIP catalogue record for this book is available at the British Library.

ISBN 978-1-913770-74-7

Typeset in Kanit.

For Gill, my soulmate and inspiration.
Thank you for always being there.

CONTENTS

INTRODUCTION

I think most of us intuitively associate wisdom with older people and the knowledge they have accumulated throughout their lives. There is, of course, some truth to that. For me though, wisdom is gained from the people you meet, the places you travel to, the situations you find yourself in, and seeing things from different perspectives.

Plus, learning from them; after all, life is one big classroom.

You can be old and not wise because you haven't learnt a thing, so you keep making the same mistakes, time and time again. You can be young and be very wise; my youngest grandson never ceases to amaze me with what he says or does.

A Google search of what is wisdom will yield numerous results, such as, *'the quality or state of being wise; knowledge of what is true or right coupled with just judgment as to action; sagacity, discernment, or insight'*.

I'll leave you to decide what is right or wrong. My first book *Mastering the Wolf* was an account of my life and career in both the British Army and the police service. It is a heady mix of light and dark which touches on some of the mistakes I have made along the way, along with the lessons I hope I have learnt.

I have had the pleasure of meeting (and working with) many colourful characters over the years. Some were the masters of one-liners, some shared words of advice, and many offered their opinions on life, love, work and more.

Many of those words have stayed with me for years.

I thought it would be fun to share them. This book contains 31 one-liners or snippets of wisdom designed as one per day for a month, with a couple of extras for good measure. Please feel free to read them at your own pace though.

WOLFIE
WISDOM

1

LOOK AFTER NUMBER ONE

As a young cop at the training school, I remember walking alone to my lessons when a guy in plain clothes stopped me and asked how long I had been in the police. My reply was in days, not weeks. In the short conversation that followed, he told me he was a detective and had been in 'the job' for years. He said, "I am going to offer you a piece of advice: Look after number one."

You may think it a selfish state of mind to have, but it is not, because unless you can look after number one, you cannot take care of anyone else.

2

YOU ONLY GET ONE CHANCE AT LIFE... LIVE IT!

I've heard this one several times and honestly cannot attribute it to one single person, but it touches me.

Loss is part of life and if you have read my book, *Mastering the Wolf*, you will know my mother was taken early, as have so many of my friends. You just do not know when your time is up.

So 'live' your life, seek out opportunities, spend time with the people you love and make the most of it – you are only here once!

3

CHIN UP, CHEST OUT, SHOULDERS BACK!

Anyone from a service background will be familiar with this. As I mention in *Mastering the Wolf*, I joined the army at the age of 16 and was brought down to earth with a bump.

This little phrase was something shouted into your face by drill sergeants or bellowed at you from across the parade ground. Discipline, pride and deportment are key facets of the Armed Forces.

Ultimately, it is about standing tall, how you carry yourself and how others perceive you. Slouch and you get noticed for the wrong reasons.

Chin up, chest out and shoulders back are also good for your posture, particularly as you get older in life.

4

LIFE AIN'T FAIR; GET OVER IT!

I am very open in my first book about seeking counselling at a point in my life where things were going badly wrong. During one of my sessions, the counsellor said, "Life isn't fair."

Like many of the one-liners in this short book, those words have never left me. We are all going to suffer at times in our life. It's wasted energy to feel sorry for yourself, so get over it, pick yourself up and move on.

The irony with this little tale is that Rachael, the lovely lady who was my counsellor, died in 2022 from a terminal illness. I was fortunate to be able to get a copy of my book to her several weeks before her passing, with a thank you note inside. A beautiful soul, and her experience epitomises this one-liner perfectly.

5

THERE IS NO TRUTH, ONLY PERSPECTIVE...

This one-liner is mostly relevant to relationships and dealing with people.

I recall it being told to me by a former police officer when I was experiencing some particularly difficult times. With relationships, there are always two sides to the story, each party believing their version of the truth.

If you rely on memories, the same is true; our recall can be affected by a host of things, which can in turn cloud judgement and decision-making.

This, in my humble opinion, is about empathy and being able to take a step back and look at different aspects of whatever you are dealing with. I hope it's helpful to you; it has been to me.

6

NEVER MENTION THE Q WORD...

Today's one-liner is Murphy's Law of Policing.

Murphy's Law says, "Anything that can go wrong will go wrong, and at the worst possible time."

One thing we were told frequently whilst on patrol (now called response policing) is the Q word... (Q is code for Quiet).

As a young PC, I made the fatal mistake of saying, "It's quiet," during a night shift at about 11 pm, and all hell broke loose. My sergeant could quite happily have flattened me, as within seconds a massive brawl broke out at a working men's club, which required a lot of help to quell.

So, if it's quiet in your life and you want to keep it that way, make the most of it and keep it to yourself!

7

I'M AFRAID IT'S A CASE OF JFDI!

Today's one-liner takes me back many years. You will doubtless be familiar with the Nike phrase 'Just Do It'.

Well, JFDI is a turn of phrase with an expletive included and often spoken with some emphasis, for example Just ****ing Do It! (The expletive being removed as I don't want to offend!)

JFDI was quoted at me when I was explaining to one of my bosses the difficulty we were having managing change in the police with a particular project. What he said was, "Well, Colin, I'm afraid it's a case of they will have to JFDI." Choice was not an option, and it wasn't a democracy.

Sometimes times are tough, and sometimes you don't want to do certain things that have to be done, so when that happens, change your mindset and think JFDI.

8

TREAT PEOPLE HOW YOU WOULD EXPECT YOUR PARENTS TO BE TREATED...

Another one I can never forget, and to the best of my recall was told to all our (very large) intake on day one at police training school by our instructors.

"Treat people how you would expect your parents to be treated, and you will not go far wrong."

Now, remember that police officers don't always meet and deal with nice people. So, I am going to factor in another piece of wisdom shared with me by one of the finest police sergeants I ever had the pleasure of working with. He said, "You can always start by being polite and up your tone if the situation doesn't work out. You cannot do it the other way around."

This is a great piece of advice which I believe served me well over the years.

9

YOU CAN PLEASE SOME OF THE PEOPLE, SOME OF THE TIME, BUT YOU CANNOT PLEASE ALL OF THE PEOPLE, ALL OF THE TIME...

I've heard this so many times over the years, and it is an important reminder to us all. It is all too easy to be a people-pleaser, but let me tell you, it does not work.

Have people-pleasing as a mindset and it will give you one big headache, particularly if you are, or aspire to be, in a leadership role.

Be yourself, be true to yourself, walk your own path, and be responsible for your actions.

10

IT'S ONLY PAIN!

My memories of this one-liner are firmly rooted in service life. As a recruit, you soon come to realise that once you join any of the armed services, you have to be broken to be rebuilt.

For example, you would be pushed to your absolute limit in physical activity, route marches, sleep deprivation, and so on, and if you showed any sense of flagging, the instructors would shout at you *"It's only pain!"* Often with a swear word or two thrown in for good measure, followed by *"It will pass!"*

Pain isn't pleasant, be it physical or emotional, and it does pass, or get less intense eventually. When the pain comes, tell yourself, it is only pain, and that you will overcome it.

11

BE LIKE A SWAN...

One of the things I struggled with in my youth was public speaking. Growing up, I was shy and reserved. I give an example in my book *Mastering the Wolf* of what happened when I joined the police.

In later years, to counter my anxieties, I put myself forward as a trainer, which involved an intensive course. One of the things we were told during the course about standing up in front of a group of people was *"Be like a Swan, effortlessly gliding across the water, but underneath your legs will be going ten to the dozen."*

I learnt that nerves were OK; you have to embrace them and treat them in your mind as excitement, and it changes the game.

Something scaring you? Be like a Swan.

12

NEVER RUN TO A FIGHT...

My first posting in the police was to the mining town of Castleford in West Yorkshire. As a naive 21-year-old probationer constable, it was often the case that the older officers would share advice with you.

The weekends were like the Wild West; men and women would flock into town, party and drink hard, and inevitably that led to a scrap somewhere.

The wisdom behind this one-liner was simple. Let those who are fighting each other tire themselves out before you get there. Rest assured, you will need all your energy when you arrive.

13

WE ARE ALL IN THE GUTTER, BUT SOME OF US ARE LOOKING AT THE STARS...

This piece of wisdom was shouted at me and a colleague by a young student after arresting her and a group of friends for possession of cannabis at a property in Leeds during the 1980s.

I laughed it off at the time and had no idea what she was talking about. I later discovered it is a quote attributed to Oscar Wilde.

Putting aside the arrest, these words are both powerful and motivating. For we all at some point in our lives will find ourselves in the proverbial gutter. When that happens, look up and find your stars. Treat them like goals and shoot for them.

14

I'VE FORGOTTEN FORGOTTEN MORE THAN WHAT YOU'VE LEARNT, KID...

Today's wisdom again dates to my early days in the police service. The old sweats, who had been around for a long time, would often say this to the probationers (those with less than two years' service).

It was in fairness a bit of a put-down but did have an element of truth to it, because there was so much to learn in 'the job' as we affectionately referred to it. Not just the laws, procedures and so on, but how society changes and how the police have to adapt very quickly.

15

YOU GET OUT WHAT YOU PUT IN...

have so many examples of this one-liner being quoted at me or overheard during conversations.

Unless you are very, very lucky, success in life, work or business does not fall into your lap. You must work hard whilst being relentless in pursuit of your goals.

Put the effort in and it will pay off; maybe not straight away, but it will eventually.

Keep going!

16

THE BEST VIEWS COME AFTER THE HARDEST CLIMBS...

This is one of my all-time favourites and I probably saw it on one of those inspirational posters somewhere, some time ago. It certainly chimed with me.

I have always enjoyed being in the mountains and the hills. I mention it in my book and can still vividly recall some of the physical challenges in Norway when being trained for Arctic Warfare. Any climb uphill is invariably hard; you get out of breath, your body can ache, and you question yourself.

But when you get to the top (providing the weather is good), the views are unequalled, and it all becomes worth it.

There are parallels in life, it will get tough at times, and it will hurt, but when you get to where you are going, it's amazing!

17

AND...
BREATHE...

recall we used to say this to each other quite often in the police, usually after a stressful event such as a difficult interview, or a member of the public that wouldn't listen to reason.

It was spoken with some exasperation most of the time, whilst flicking the eyes skywards; you know the feeling, I'm sure. It's applicable across all areas of life.

I have since discovered there is some science to breathing properly though.

If something stressful is happening, an argument, a dispute, or things not going right, then stop. Take a deep breath through your nose and out through your mouth. That rapidly beating heart will begin to slow and you can start to think more rationally.

It's an exercise you can practice at any time PLUS it is completely FREE!

Try this: breathe in through the nose for the count of four, and breathe out through the mouth for the count of four. Do it for a few minutes; it works!

18

FIVE MINUTES BEFORE A PARADE...

Anyone who has served time in the armed services will be very familiar with this one-liner.

Strolling down to that very first parade on the 10th September 1975 without a care in the world, many of us got a rude awakening. An 0800hrs parade meant being there at least five minutes early – anything less and you were either doing press-ups or running around the parade square, and if a repeat offender, sent to see the Sergeant Major.

It instilled in me self-discipline, and I quickly ensured I was on that parade square early. In later life, I was always well before time for my shifts in the police. I hate being late, something my wife and family take great delight in taking the mickey out of me for.

If I am honest, I have wasted days of my life being too early for appointments, flights, trains and assorted events. But I would still rather do that than arrive flustered.

I also feel strongly that if you have an appointment with someone, then it is disrespectful to them if you are not there on time. I must admit though, that if someone keeps me waiting, it is a niggle.

19

LEAD BY EXAMPLE...

Many years ago, in my mission to be promoted in the police, I attended an Action Centred Leadership course, the first time I had been exposed to any formal training in management.

One of the very first things we were all taught was to 'lead by example'. In fairness, this was not the first time I had heard or experienced it, but it was reinforced throughout the two days.

Looking back, the people who have made the greatest impression on me are those that did exactly that. They set an example in everything they did, the way they talked to their peers, and the people that they managed. But also in their appearance, bearing, punctuality, desire to succeed and respect for those in less senior positions.

I am not a political animal, but we have been set some atrocious examples of how 'not' to lead by certain individuals in power, and the net result is mistrust of authority.

Trust is earned and in my humble opinion, you set the standards as a leader. If they are low, then you will not get the best out of your people. Keep them high and you can take the world on.

If you are in the fortunate position of being in power (of any sort), please lead by example.

20

YOU'VE GOT TO CRACK A FEW EGGS TO MAKE AN OMELETTE...

This amused me when I first heard it during quite a tense meeting. I confess I had to look down to conceal a wry smile. The senior officer that said it was doubtless the best boss I ever had. He had a way of defusing a situation with humour which almost always led to a pivotal moment.

Despite the humour, he also acknowledged that mistakes would get made. The important thing is to learn from them. Just like life, rarely do we get things right the first time.

So don't be worried about breaking a few eggs along the way.

21

SOME PEOPLE WANT IT TO HAPPEN, SOME WISH IT WOULD HAPPEN, AND OTHERS MAKE IT HAPPEN...

Have you watched the film *Air*? It's about Nike and its relentless pursuit to sign Michael Jordan. It is a truly brilliant account of a business's resilience, drive and determination to get their man.

Today's quote is attributed to Michael Jordan. I have used it for years on one of my online accounts.

With 40-plus of work life behind me, I have met many people who 'want' or 'wish' things to happen but don't have the drive or the will to get things off the ground. I must be honest and say they frustrate the hell out of me. Things rarely fall into your lap. You have to work hard to be successful.

I have been privileged to have worked with some wonderful men and women who made it happen, and they are inspiring. We can't all be Jordan, but we can show up and do our best every day.

22

THINK OF YOUR MIND LIKE A PARACHUTE. IT WORKS BEST WHEN IT'S OPEN...

Once qualified as a police trainer, I had an awakening. The course itself was intensive, and we spent a lot of time understanding human behaviour, how there are different approaches to teaching, and the importance of adapting your style to suit others.

This quote came up quite a bit during my time in that role and it is so true across life. Without an open parachute, you will come down to earth with a bump. Be open-minded, consider other perspectives, and you will benefit and grow.

23

IT'S GOOD TO TALK...

Now this small nugget of wisdom may sound a little clichéd, but it has power and meaning.

Being brought up in the sixties, joining the forces as a boy and then onto the police, talking about stuff was not the 'done' thing. By 'stuff', I mean your concerns, worries, fears, troubles – in fact, all those emotional things that blokes don't generally like talking about. It's perceived as a weakness.

Eventually, that strategy tends to blow up in your face. You would have to read my first book to find out more.

So, my advice is if you are feeling down, worried or anxious, find someone you can confide in and chat to them. It's good to talk, trust me.

24

ASSUME NOTHING, BELIEVE NOBODY, CHECK EVERYTHING...

ABC is a maxim that police officers, particularly detectives, are taught very early on in their careers. It's an essential tool in the box.

What does it mean?

Never **A**ssume anything! You know what they say about making an ASS out of U and ME...

Believe nobody! If you are a police officer, ex-police officer or have a police officer in the family, then you'll know what I mean. Asking questions, desperate to prove a point, ferreting around for answers, and so on.

Check everything! Investigations can be complex and rest upon the smallest piece of information, a vital aspect of police work.

ABC works 'at work', but can creep into our personal lives; it can make you untrusting, argumentative and deeply suspicious. You must keep that in check.

I still investigate for a living, but use a slightly different ABC now: **A**ssume nothing (essential), **B**elieve nothing (not nobody) UNTIL you **C**heck everything.

That works for me and brings back the balance, though I have to be honest – the old ABC does creep back in from time to time...!

25

WE DON'T HAVE MUCH MONEY, BUT WE DO SEE LIFE...

Not so much a quote today but something that a very good friend of mine, Geoff, used to say frequently. Geoff was my first wife's uncle. He and his wife Kath pretty much adopted us when we arrived in Castleford, Yorkshire, for my first police posting.

Both were kindness personified; they took care of me and my family when times were hard. Geoff and I would go walking in the Yorkshire Dales from time to time and he would always make me laugh. He also seemed to know everybody, once even at the top of Pen-y-Ghent!

"We don't have much money, but we do see life", was one of his favourite sayings. The truth is neither of us had much money, but we had some great times. Times that I will remember for the rest of my time on this earth.

Sadly, Geoff passed some years ago. His saying always reminds me that it's not money that makes you rich, rather it is what you do during your time here and whom you choose to spend it with.

26

A POLICEMAN WITHOUT A PEN IS LIKE A FAIRY WITHOUT A WAND...

OK, first things first, this quote is not gender correct, but it originates from the 1980s when I first heard it. Nowadays, I accept it would be a police 'officer'.

Writing reports was something of an art form for me and I struggled with it when I joined the service. I mention in *Mastering the Wolf* that my reports for summons (which were mostly handwritten then) were submitted and came back time and time again from the process sergeant. The role of the process sergeant was to ensure that anything submitted for prosecution was of the highest standard and they had no mercy, particularly for officers who were young in service.

Evidence had to be presented properly and you had to work on the 'points to prove'; anything less was a failure. So, the magic had to happen on paper, otherwise your case was doomed to fail.

I think many officers of that era loathed process sergeants, but they were an essential part of a system that worked. Sadly, they were eventually replaced by the introduction of administrative support units, where some would say the magic and quality were lost forever.

I like to think I am still using my wand, albeit in a different way.

27

BELIEVE THE UNBELIEVABLE...

Now this quote may sound similar to one I have used before about ABC, but the context is slightly different.

Between 1995 and 1999, I was a detective sergeant supervising a busy Child Protection Unit in Leeds. I worked with, and learnt from, some amazing individuals and it was the most rewarding time of my police career. But, at times, also the most harrowing.

Adults do the most appalling things to children, and it is hard for outsiders to comprehend; some prefer to claim it is fantasy. During my time working with the units, I was one of several officers that attended a presentation by the late Ray Wyre. Mr Wyre founded the Gracewell Clinic, the first residential clinic for the counselling of child abusers, and was famed for working with sex offenders, notably Robert Black who abducted, sexually assaulted and murdered several young girls, including Sarah Harper, from Morley in Leeds.

In closing his presentation, he said, when dealing with child abuse, "Believe the Unbelievable", words that have never left me. We were, after all, often dealing with young children who had no voice and had been harmed in all manner of ways by adults. We needed to do our best for them, and these few words are worth remembering.

28

WORK HARD, PLAY HARD...

This one most definitely has its origins in my service days. Be it training, exercises or real-world deployments, you were expected to give 100% at all times. Excuses were not tolerated. The play-hard element was access to all manner of sporting activities, or, it has to be said, drinking to excess!

I'm going to add another layer today though. My parents and my stepfather (who has played a large part in my life) worked hard, each in their own way, setting a great example for me. My father was a bank messenger; he worked all hours but was always immaculately dressed in a suit and tie. My mother looked after her four children, washing, cleaning, cooking and holding down other jobs. Likewise, my stepfather worked on the land and did part-time work at a farm as well.

Did they play hard? Yes, they did. My father loved to play and watch his football, my mum liked a party and baking wonderful food, and my stepfather just loved keeping my mum happy. They were a joy together.

Nowadays, it's popular to call this work-life balance. It's good to work hard, but don't live to work. Work to live, enjoy the time away from your job and do what makes you happy.

29

YOU ARE ONLY RESPONSIBLE FOR FIFTY PER CENT OF A RELATIONSHIP...

This quote should be read in the context of the relationship between couples. I first heard it during counselling sessions.

I was in the midst of an awful relationship at the time. Things at home were terrible, and it was impacting my work and family. They truly were some of the worst times of my life. If it has happened to you, then it may be the case that you blame yourself; I know I did.

I questioned my sanity, found it difficult to escape, and wherever possible, worked away from home. It was a recipe for disaster and not pleasant for either side.

It wasn't until my counsellor told me this about responsibility that I realised we were both to blame, it wasn't just one of us. I also knew if we stayed together, it would only get much worse. Things ultimately came to a head and that is detailed in my first book.

If it is you making all the effort in a relationship, or if it is you not putting all the effort in, then the balance is out of kilter. It has to be 50/50; nothing else works.

30

BLINK AND YOU'LL MISS IT...

I've heard this on numerous occasions and the meaning should be obvious. Perhaps you may be thinking of fast cars, motorbikes, etc., etc. However, I am talking about life.

I am a member of two Facebook groups that relate to my previous career, one from my time in the army, and the other in the police. It seems that every time I check in to read posts, someone has passed, often from a terminal illness.

Make the most of every single moment of your life, because as you get older it seems the days go by quicker. You never know if, or when, your number is up, so please don't blink and miss it.

Colin Tansley

31

DON'T LOOK BACK... YOU'RE NOT GOING THAT WAY...

64

We can all be guilty of beating ourselves up when things don't go right or we make mistakes. The thing is, mistakes are a part of life, and if we didn't make them, we wouldn't learn.

I am having trouble remembering who first said this to me, but I am almost certain it was a police supervisor many years ago. It is such a great reminder that I had it inscribed on a tankard for my son.

Put another way, this quote means don't dwell on the past. We all mess up and if you've learnt from a mistake, then you demonstrate you have by not making it again.

BONUS

32

YOU ARE WHAT YOU EAT...

first heard this quote when I worked on a public order unit (Task Force) in the police. One of the sergeants was purported to be ex-Special Forces and was keen on fitness and health.

Being younger, I just thought he was a little obsessed if I'm honest.

It's only as I have got older that the importance of good food and nutrition has become important to me. I harbour a sweet tooth, probably inherited from my late mother who loved a cake. But it is important to ensure that your diet includes fruit, vegetables and fresh food because they have an abundance of benefits.

You have one body and it is important to take good care of it with the fuel you consume.

33

BE GRATEFUL...

If you had mentioned this one to me 12 months ago, I would have dismissed it out of hand. My inner cynic would have come into play.

Then I went to an event on the Isle of Man hosted by a company that comprised of several ex-service people. They talked about the power of our thoughts and how we can make use of our inner strength to put us in a better frame of mind.

We were set a 30-day challenge, including cold showers, which I was already doing. But another one was to write down each day three things that you are grateful for. I was puzzled why you would want to do it, but I am open to trying new things.

It was a struggle at first, but the guys said to think about the simplest things to get you started. Your food, your home, your partner, your children, waking up in the morning, and so on.

It's been over a year now, and each day I now record one thing I am grateful for. I often look back at what I have written. Why do it? It makes you realise just how rich your life is, and it puts you in a positive mindset and as a recovering cynic, I need that.

Try it, you might like it.

LAST WORD

I hope you enjoyed my Wolfie Wisdom. The truth is I could have continued writing for so much longer; every so often I remember even more.

I would remind you of what I said at the beginning of this little book.

Life is one big classroom.

You are going to make mistakes, no one is perfect, and the most important thing is to learn from them. My late counsellor Rachael read me these powerful words some years ago.

"I walk down the street.
There is a deep hole in the sidewalk.
I fall in.
I am lost... I am helpless.
It isn't my fault.
It takes forever to find a way out.

I walk down the same street.
There is a deep hole in the sidewalk.

I pretend I don't see it.
I fall in again.
I can't believe I am in the same place.
But it isn't my fault.
It still takes me a long time to get out.

I walk down the same street.
There is a deep hole in the sidewalk.
I see it is there.
I still fall in. It's a habit.
My eyes are open.
I know where I am.
It is my fault. I get out immediately.

I walk down the same street.
There is a deep hole in the sidewalk.
I walk around it.

I walk down another street."

— Portia Nelson,
There's a Hole in My Sidewalk:
The Romance of Self–Discovery

In my humble opinion, accumulating wisdom comes from listening, reflecting, being honest with yourself and accepting you may have to change. I know that I am not the same person

I was 10, 20 or 30 years ago, and I am OK with that. I've been fortunate to have met and worked with some phenomenal people over the years who have shared their knowledge with me. Many have passed, but they live on in this little book.

ABOUT THE AUTHOR

Colin Tansley, a former soldier and police officer, has transitioned from a dedicated career in public service, to become an accomplished entrepreneur. His journey began with a foundation in the military, where he honed his skills as a Royal Signals Army Apprentice over two years before embarking on deployments both domestically and abroad. Notably, he served in Northern Ireland during the late seventies, contributing to the complex landscape of that era.

Later moving into law enforcement, Colin embraced diverse roles encompassing uniformed duties, undercover work, child protection initiatives, training, and managerial responsibilities. Through first-hand experiences, he gained profound insights into pivotal moments, such as the upheavals of the early eighties, the miner's strike of 1984, combating child abuse, and tackling organised crime.

Colin's professional journey also took him across borders, as he shared his expertise globally, offering guidance and support while even volunteering in post–war Iraq. Beyond his career, Colin is a devoted father, stepfather, and grandfather, having faced and overcome numerous personal and professional trials.

Endowed with qualities of approachability, determination, and unwavering motivation, Colin is celebrated for his inherent ability to connect with people. His unwavering commitment to investigative work, risk management, safeguarding vulnerable enterprises, and challenging inequity remains at the forefront of his work. Through his venture, Intelect Group, he continues to champion these principles, leaving a lasting impact.

Adding to his multifaceted accomplishments, Colin is also a published author, having penned *Mastering the Wolf: One man's story of emotional enlightenment* (2022, Book Brilliance Publishing) which delves into a personal journey of self-discovery, resonating with readers on a profound level.

In essence his life story is a testament to resilience, empathy, and unyielding commitment to making a positive difference in the lives of others.

Keep in touch with the author:

Twitter: @author_colin

Facebook: facebook.com/
MTW22.2.22/

https://colintansley.com/

hello@colintansley.com

linkedin.com/in/colintansleyintelect

www.ingramcontent.com/pod-product-compliance
Lightning Source LLC
Chambersburg PA
CBHW071245020426
42333CB00015B/1635